This book belongs to:

____

Made in the USA
Monee, IL
15 July 2022

99771827R00061